MW00791353

"Behold the Handmaid of the Lord!"

MOTHERS' MANUAL

Helps for Mothers and Expectant Mothers

by A. Francis Coomes, S.J.

Illustrated by
Mary Katherine Murphy

William J. Hirten C°., Inc.
6100   17th   Avenue
Brooklyn, N.Y. 11204

IMPRIMI POTEST
   Gerald R. Sheahan, S.J.
   Praep. Prov. Missourianae

NIHIL OBSTAT
   William M. Drumm
   Censor Librorum

IMPRIMATUR
   † John J. Carberry
   Archiepiscopus Sti. Ludovici
   Sti. Ludovici die 8 Februarii 1970

(fifth revision)

© Copyright 1973, 1984
Rev. A. Francis Coomes, S.J.

CONTENTS

1

FOR TIMES OF SPECIAL PROBLEMS

BLESSINGS AND FEASTS

COUNSELS AND HELPS FOR A WIFE AND MOTHER

INTRODUCTION

By a loving providence of almighty God, all motherhood has been elevated to receive a new status through the motherhood of Mary.

This relationship in grace of every motherhood with Mary's special motherhood assures all mothers that Mary has a particular regard for each of them.

The prayer aids and directives of this little manual are presented to help today's mothers in realizing and fulfilling the dignity of their state. It is hoped that these offerings will be instrumental in bringing mothers closer to the heart of Christ and will effectively join them in unity of prayer with Mary, and so help them realize something of the beautiful image of the Mother of Christ in the motherhood with which they have been blessed.

5

MORNING PRAYER

My Jesus, I offer this day to you —
all my prayers, works, joys, and
sufferings — and, through you, I
make this offering to our Father in
heaven. Be with me through this
whole day in all its particulars, and
assist me that it may become a
worthy offering in every way.

Be close to me in all I think and say
and do. Direct your Spirit to speak
to me and guide me — and help me
to listen attentively when he does
speak ... so that, in my response,
your thoughts may become more
surely my thoughts, and your ways
may become my ways; so that my
judgments may accord with your
judgments, and that the sentiments
of my heart may be most like your

very own; so that my conversation with others may be conversation I may ask you to share with us, and that my works may be works I may ask you to approve.

Help me to have the practical wisdom to look to your Mother from time to time, as I go about the duties of my day, in an effort to find the grace of a better way in my motherhood; for she is the perfect example of all virtues and is your loving gift to us as a perfect model for all motherhood.

May I know the continued grace to work *with* you in all I do, and not merely *for* you ... so that my day may become a perfect offering — lived with you and in you and through you — to be presented to our Father in joy and love.

8

FOR A HAPPY MARRIED LIFE

Lord, bless and preserve my cherished husband, whom you have given to me. Let his life be long and blessed, comfortable and holy; let me ever be a blessing and a comfort to him, a sharer in all his sorrows, a consolation in all the accidents and trials of life. Make me forever lovable in his eyes and forever dear to him. Unite his heart to mine in fondest love and holiness, and mine to him in all sweetness and charity. Keep me from all ungentleness; make me humble, yet strong and helpful, that we may delight in each other according to your blessed word. May both of us rejoice in you, having our portion in the love and service of God forever. Amen.

In preparation

for

Motherhood

and for

young Motherhood

TO HAVE A CHILD

Mother of Christ, you know, as no other mother can, the high dignity of motherhood. You know how immensely great is the privilege to call into this world a tiny soul destined to praise God forever in heaven.

This is the privilege I now seek, Mary!

Confidently I beg you to assist me, for I know that motherhood is so precious in your sight. And confidently, too, I hope for this blessing through your divine Son, since Jesus is the lover of the little children and has said that we should allow them to come to him.

It is for this blessing that I beg you to join to my petitions your own holy intercession, that I might be

Mother of the Infant Christ,
Speak to Jesus for me.

privileged to bring to Jesus a little one such as he so dearly loves, that he may bless it, that he may bless me, also, in my motherhood, and that he may then make us both grow in the wonders of his divine life.

Mother of Mothers,
Pray for me!

THANKSGIVING FOR CONCEPTION

I rejoice in my conception, Lord, and I give thanks that my husband and I have been chosen to share in the work of your love. In your great and tender wisdom, you do not wish to multiply the human family by your power alone. You allow us, your humble creatures, to share in your creative might. The soul of our tiny babe will be your work alone;

its body will be your work and ours, too, for we are its father and mother. But, soul and body, it will be our possession forever as well as yours. May this child ever remind us that you and we have worked lovingly side by side.

How can I ever return sufficient thanks for this great honor? I offer humbly my homage and heartfelt devotion.

THANKSGIVING FOR MOTHERHOOD

Accept my humble gratitude, most holy Trinity!

Thanks be to the Father, who manifested unlimited power within me by drawing forth from nothingness another human soul and giving it to my care.

Thanks be to the Son, who has revealed his eternal wisdom within me by fashioning another flame of human life so delicate that it can neither be seen nor heard, so strong that it will live forever.

Thanks be to the Holy Spirit, who has shown his everlasting love within me by forming another human heart to spend its days on earth in praising God and returning love for love.

Omnipotent triune God — Father, Son, and Holy Spirit — receive my humble thanks and my undying devotion.

FOR AN EXPECTANT MOTHER

Dearest Mary, I look to you now for the help of your maternal love.

You understand my trials as an expectant mother. You bore Jesus in your womb. You know the doubts and anxieties that beset me; you know the bodily suffering I endure. Like you, may I turn all these sorrows into joy. You overcame anxiety by a loving trust in God; you overcame doubt by gentle resignation to his will. Your motherhood lifted your mind above earth and kept it close to God.

So speak to Jesus now with me, beloved Mother, as I seek prayerfully to learn to bear the trials of motherhood with joy.

Mother of Perpetual Help,
Pray for me!

THOUGHTS FOR AN EXPECTANT MOTHER

What must have been your joy, Mary, when the angel announced that you were to become a mother, the true mother of God's own Son! You were so happy — yes, far happier even than I am, and your heart burst forth in a song of praise: "My soul magnifies the Lord, and my spirit rejoices in God my savior."
Did you often think of the wonderful Son whom you would bear? Mary, think now of our dear child, my husband's and mine, and watch over it always. During those months before the first Christmas morn, how reverently you guarded that precious treasure within your body. Now I carry within me a precious treasure,

our child. Your son was the son of God, and our child will soon become an adopted child of God when the waters of baptism make its soul godlike and beautiful.

Mary, thank God for us and with us; thank him for all his goodness to us. And pray with us that we may know how to care for the child that he has given us. Join your prayers with ours that I may be a good mother, as you were, and that my husband may be a good father with a fatherhood patterned as closely as possible on the perfect fatherhood of God.

And, Mary, let me ask for one thing more. Since your boy was the best and most lovable of children, turn your motherly care to our child now so that it may grow up to be as much as possible like Jesus, and like yourself, his mother. This is the grace that I desire most of all.

Tell me, virgin blest, what were your thoughts when you contemplated your God and Maker.
Who came from heaven to earth to dwell in you.

TO NURSE A CHILD

Holy Mary, you remember devoutly how as a young mother you pressed the divine Jesus tenderly to your breast. You were not then denied that precious privilege of motherhood, to nourish the life you had brought into this world.
Dear Mother of Mothers, I beg you to speak to God with me now to

obtain the privilege that I too may so nourish the child to whom I shall soon give birth. May I know this fulness of the office of holy motherhood. And ask with me, too, holy Mother, that, in the fulfillment of this blessed office which God has so beautifully ordained, I shall be closely drawn to my child with the tenderest mother love and that by this bond of affection I shall likewise be better able to nourish the soul of my little one with the holy truths of faith, so that my child may serve its Creator with a strong body and an upright mind in fidelity and love.

Mother of Mothers,
Pray for me!

FOR A HAPPY DELIVERY

Lord Jesus Christ, who said, "Allow the little children to come to me, for the kingdom of heaven is for such," I thank you with all my heart for the great and holy privilege you have granted me in calling me to present you with a little child, so precious in your sight. I praise and bless your divine goodness which has conferred this supreme favor on me, and I acknowledge myself altogether unworthy of this holy gift.

I bless, too, your divine goodness for giving me such a sweet and holy patroness and protectress in your mother, the model and exaltation of all Christian motherhood.

Dear Jesus, I beg you to be mindful of the prayers and intercession of your immaculate mother in my behalf; heed her petitions for me and, as you have so blessed me in this pregnancy, mercifully grant the happy delivery which I now ask through her, my patroness, our Lady of Happy Delivery. Amen.

FOR A MOTHER'S DOCTOR

Lord Jesus Christ, lover of little children, grant your abundant blessings on my doctor. For even more important than the task of preserving life is his task of bringing that life into this world. Give my doctor a deep appreciation of the work that he performs. May he ever know how precious that duty is in your sight. Guide his hands at all times, and may all their work be done to your

Mother Most Pure

honor. May he ever regard his office as a sacred trust received from you. And finally, may he one day know your rich rewards for having striven earnestly and faithfully to help little children to come to you according to your desires. Amen.

FOR THE TRUE SPIRIT OF MOTHERHOOD

Mary, my mother, join me now in a mother's prayer that, through the special graces of motherhood, my little child may instruct me in the ways of God: that its innocent eyes may speak to me of the spotless holiness of Jesus; that its open smile may continually remind me of the great love God has for his creatures; that its helplessness may teach me the unbounded power of God; and that its first feeble efforts to speak may tell me of God's wisdom.

Pray with me now that its complete trust in me may lead me to a like confidence in God, and that its simple affection for me may bring me to a greater love for him.

And so, in all these things, may I grow in a greater appreciation of my holy motherhood, and day by day reflect more faithfully the radiant beauty manifest in your motherhood, which God gave us as the model of all Christian motherhood.

Mother of Mothers,
Pray for me!

FOR THE GRACES OF MOTHERHOOD

Powerful is your intercession with God, Mary, for you are his mother.

Tender, too, is your love for us, for you are our mother.

Confidently, then, I come to you as a child, poor and needy, to seek your aid and protection.

In every trial of motherhood, I beg your aid.

For the grace of a happy delivery, I come to you.

For your holy assistance in guarding and directing each tiny soul with which God entrusts me, I call to you.

In every sorrow that comes to me in my motherhood, I confide in you.

That I may have strength to bear

cheerfully all the pains and the hardships of motherhood, I lean on you.

That the sweetness of motherhood may not through my neglect be embittered in later years by pains of regret, I trust in you.

That the will of God may always be fulfilled in me through each act of my motherhood, little and great, I beg your aid.

Never forsake me, dear Mother, my hope, my consolation, my confidence, and my trust, but ever be at my side to aid and protect me, your needy child. Amen.

Mother of Love, of Sorrow, and of Mercy,
Pray for us!

THANKSGIVING

Mary, I am so happy! I, too, am a mother. Thank you for joining me in my petitions to your divine son, dear Mother of Happy Delivery.
You were with me in my Bethlehem. Thank you. I know you are with me now in my Nazareth. Thank you, thank you.

For

Motherhood

and

Married

Life

PRAISE

It is truly fitting, Mary, that we should honor you.

For God chose to honor you by making you his mother.

The prophets of old spoke of you with their fairest praises, the glory of Israel and of all womankind.

The angel bowed in reverence as he addressed you who were chosen to be God's mother.

And all generations have called you blessed.

So joyfully, Mary, we praise you:

We praise you in your purity, far more radiant than that of the brightest seraphim and cherubim.

We praise you in your maternity, in which you were privileged to nourish your God and creator at your breast.

Immaculate Heart of Mary,
Pray for us now and at the hour of our death!

We praise you in your virginity, which you kept so preciously together with your holy maternity.

We praise you in the honor which through you has been given to holy motherhood throughout the ages.

We praise you in the courage your pure and holy example has given to Christian mothers in a sinful world.

We praise you, too, in your motherhood, which by God's decree has made you our mother and us your children.

Yes, always and at all times and in all places will we praise and honor and bless you, as it is proper to do, holy Mother of God, ever-blessed virgin, mother of fair love! Amen.

FOR FIDELITY IN MARRIED LIFE

Lord Jesus Christ, by your presence at the wedding feast, you blessed the state of holy matrimony; and by a special token of your love and favor you have raised marriage to the dignity of a sacrament. Grant now that I, together with my husband, may be ever faithful to the marriage vows we have pledged.

May all our living bring us closer together in mutual love and in love for you.

May no act of ours be ever unworthy in your sight.

May we never forget the ends for which matrimony has been instituted. And especially may we never, through selfishness, defile ourselves and our love, by unlawful acts of any sort that may displease you.

Teach us to trust in you, to receive the little children you send us, and to offer them back to receive your love. Grant us the spiritual and temporal means to rear these children properly. And thus may we deserve your favors, which we seek in our marriage.

May every expression of our love for one another be united to our love for you.

FOR ONE'S HUSBAND

Lord God, loving father of us all, guide and instruct my husband in your ways that he may be a good earthly father to our children.

Help him to be wise and prudent in carrying out your designs for him as a father, and aid him that in all his ways his inspiration and example will direct our children's thoughts to you.

Grant him patience in carrying out the difficult and burdensome task of being a good father.

Teach him a strength and firmness that is tempered with gentleness and is never harsh or forbidding.

Teach him to be kind without being yielding or indulgent.

Give him the understanding that a father should have — an understanding that will invite the confidence of his children.

Give him the cheerful strength that is so often needed in times of trial; and may his love for our children, and my love for him, sustain him in these times of stress.

Give him a childlike trust in you, and may that trust in you be rewarded by a mirroring of your fatherhood in him. And so may his children know an increase of joy and love as they are brought closer to you through him. Amen.

FOR UNITY OF FAITH

Lord God, according to your holy designs you have ordained that in matrimony man and wife shall be so closely united as to become as "one flesh."
Grant now that my husband and I may be closely united in all things according to your holy law.
Grant us your abundant graces that we may enjoy the blessing of being joined by a common faith. You

know what it would mean to me if we could share completely the same religious views and convictions, if we could be united closely in the same religious practices and observances. You know what it would mean if we could share the same belief in the sacraments and have the same understanding of them and the same love for them.

That this may be realized according to your holy ways, let me never falter in my own personal obligations and in my observances of all that is required by your law of love. Bestow, in your mercy, your bounteous graces now so that one day, as completely united as possible in this life, we may both approach in joy your communion banquet and there receive together your blessing and your love.

CONSECRATION OF A CHILD TO MARY

Holy Mary, mother of God and mother of all the faithful, I place my little child under your motherly protection. To you I completely consecrate my child, body and soul. Take it under your care and keep it always. Protect it in its infancy and keep it sound in body and mind. Guard its youth and keep its heart pure, its thoughts ever holy and directed to God and the things of God. Protect it always throughout life — in its joys and sorrows, in its successes and failures, in its dealings with others. Always and in all things be a true mother to it, Mary, and preserve it. I commend it entirely to you. Remember, Mother Mary, that through this act of consecration it becomes in a special way your child as well as mine; guard it and keep it as your very own. Amen.

The angels of the little ones ever behold the face of the Father in heaven:

May the spirits of evil never have dominion over them!

FOR A GROWING INFANT

Tender Mother of the infant Christ, my child is gaining every week. Thank you for the mother's concern you share with me. Nourish my baby always with your motherly care: speak to God with me and ask him to give this little one strong limbs and a healthy body; keep your mother's eye on it asleep and awake, so that my child, as yours, may grow in wisdom and age and grace with God and men.

FOR PROTECTION OF ONE'S CHILDREN

Holy Mother Mary, by virtue of your divine motherhood you have become mother of us all. I place the dear ones God has given me under your loving protection. Be a protecting mother to my children. Guard their bodies and keep their thoughts ever holy in the sight of their creator and God. Guard their hearts and keep them pure and strong and happy in the love of God. Guard always their souls, and preserve in them faithfully the glorious image of God they received in Baptism. Always, Mother, protect them and keep them under your motherly care. Supply in your all-wise motherhood for my poor human deficiencies and protect them from all evil. Amen.

Queen of the Most Holy Family, Pray for us!

FOR A CHILD'S VOCATION TO RELIGIOUS OR PRIESTLY LIFE

Holy Mother Mary, through you I consecrate my dear child [*mention the child's name*] to the God of all life, who has given him [her] to me. Through you, I make this humble petition that, as God has so graciously given, so he may see fit to receive again my child in the closest possible dedication to his holy service. With a submissive spirit, I freely and gladly accept all the sacrifices that shall be asked of me in such a dedication. In it I shall feel that my motherhood has received its most sublime consecration, for I know that motherhood can be crowned with no higher success than in the giving and directing of souls to follow God's call in intimate love and service of him.

For my child, Mary, I beg the happiness and grace of this special dedication; for myself, the grace never to retract the precious gift that I now so gladly offer.

Queen of Virgins,
Pray for us!

DEDICATION OF A FAMILY TO MARY

(St. Alphonsus Liguori)

Blessed and immaculate Virgin, our queen and mother, you are the refuge and consolation of all those who are in need. I bow in humility before you and with my family choose you for my lady, mother, and advocate with God. I dedicate myself, and all who belong to me, forever to your service and beg you, dear mother of God, to receive us into the number of your servants. Take us all under your protection. Graciously aid us now in life and still more at the hour of death.

Mother of Mercy, I choose you lady and queen of my whole house, my relatives, my interests, and all my affairs. Take care of them; intercede for them all as it pleases you. Bless me and all my family, and do not permit any of us to offend your Son. Defend us in temptations; deliver us from doubts; console us in afflictions; be with us in sickness, and especially in the hour of death. Do not permit the devil to glory in having in his chains any of us who are now consecrated to you; but grant that we may come to you in heaven to thank you, and together with you praise and love our redeemer, Jesus, for all eternity.

THANKSGIVING FOR A HAPPY FAMILY

Blessed Queen of the most Holy Family and Queen of chaste family life, I beg you to join me in thanking your divine Son for the abundant blessings bestowed upon our happy family.

For the motherhood with which my marriage has been so graciously blessed, help me to thank him.

For the protecting hand which has guarded us against the evils that might have befallen us; for the healing hand that has restored us in our sickness; for the consoling hand that has soothed us in our moments of sorrow; for the sustaining hand that has steadied us when trials weighed us down; for the joys that have so brightened our lives; and for the holy peace that has been granted us — for these and all the precious blessings, spiritual and temporal, that have been bestowed upon us, I beg you to offer with us praise with thanksgiving.

And for the future, Mary, I humbly trust in the gracious assistance of your Son, at your motherly intercession, for myself and for each member of my family. Speak to him, for us and with us, that his assistance may continue daily throughout life — and especially that it may be our great consolation and confidence in the hour of our death.

Virgin Mary, Mother of Jesus,
Teach us to be saints!

FOR THE CONFIDENCE OF A CHILD

Mary, pray with me to obtain the gift that I may have the confidence of my child [children]. As you know, a mother needs this confidence in order to guide her children properly. When there are difficulties, or problems, or troubles, may they be shared with me trustingly, that I may more readily perform a mother's task of helping her child.

And, Mother most prudent, when this confidence is shown, obtain the grace that I may know how to help and instruct my child; that I may not only have the wisdom and prudence which is needed then to direct my child, but that I may also have the courage to say in a way that will be truly helpful the things my child should know. Be to me a mother of good counsel and, through the grace you can bring, direct me at all times in the responsibilities of my holy office of motherhood. Amen.

Seat of Wisdom,
Pray for me!

FOR GRACE
TO CORRECT A CHILD PROPERLY

Dear God, in giving me the great gift of motherhood, you have also conferred on me the sacred and weighty responsibility of patterning my child according to the model of your divine Son. May I not shirk my duty of correction, and may I fulfill this duty according to your holy will. May I realize that in administering correction I am taking your place, speaking for you; and may my corrections be such as to be worthy of this trust. May I never correct or punish a child of mine while I am angry but learn to correct in a calm, motherly manner and to administer punishment with a gentle firmness born of tender mother love rather than with any excitement of passion. May I learn to pray to you for light before I give correction or punishment — for light to guide me so that such acts of mine may be according to your holy will and in each case bring my child closer to me and both the child and myself closer to you.

FOR A CHRISTIAN ATMOSPHERE IN THE HOME

Lord Jesus Christ, you are the way and the truth and the life; and it is by following you that we will most surely find the way to our Father in heaven.

Help me, instructed by you and your example, to create a truly Christian atmosphere in our home.

May there be in all things a deep and true family life in our home — and a family life patterned after the holy family at Nazareth.

May you always be a guest at our activities, our conversations, our recreations — in a home that is truly and meaningfully centered around you.

May your picture and that of your Mother on our walls be treasured reminders of your love for us and a token of our love for you.

May the Word of God, and other books and literature that tell us of you, lead us to a closer knowledge of you and be welcomed and read by every member of the family.

May the thoughts expressed in our home be uncomplaining — at one with your thoughts and those of your holy Church.

May there be a deep respect for all things holy, and may my children learn from me and from their father a love of family prayer and of the sacraments.

May charity of speech reign in our home.

Teach us a tolerance for our neighbors that will be free from all littleness — and free from all prejudice based on race or religion.

May our ways be ever gracious in imitation of your own; and may we show a special regard for the aged, the underprivileged, the handicapped, the infirm.

And, in all the things that I expect

of my children and that I want to characterize our home, let me ever be a convincing example. May my words be always words that I may invite you to utter with me; my thoughts always thoughts that I may ask you to think with me; the feelings I make my own ever be feelings I may ask you to entertain with me; may the interpretations and judgments I make be such that I may expect you to share them with me.

So in all things may I, together with my family, be so directed by the inspirations of your grace that we may be completely one in you.

FOR THE RELIGIOUS EDUCATION OF ONE'S CHILDREN

Most loving Jesus, I realize motherhood is a sacred trust. Let me not be neglectful of my duty. I know that proper religious education is of supreme importance and that, compared to it, all other learning is of little worth. I appreciate, too, that it is a serious and grave obligation for a Christian mother to strive generously and perseveringly to obtain a good religious education for her children.

Let me not be too selfish to make the necessary sacrifices. Rather let me generously and bravely strive to obtain for them the religious education which you desire. May I always remember that I shall have to give an account to you for every soul entrusted to me; and, remembering this, may I generously fulfill that most important duty of any mother — to afford the proper spiritual instruction for her child.

Heart of Jesus, fountain of all knowledge,
Have mercy on us!

FOR A CHILD'S SUCCESS IN STUDIES

Father of lights and of all true wisdom, I humbly recommend to you the success of my child in the pursuit of learning. Mercifully grant the measure of success that it will be good for him [her] to achieve. And thus may there be a genuine sense of fulfillment as a result of efforts made.

May all knowledge attained be tempered by humility. Grant that my child's endeavors may always be guided by a sense of solid values, and help me to instill these values. And so may all his [her] striving for knowledge be made, not with the aim of surpassing others or of making vain show of ability, but rather as a worthy return to you of the talents that you have bestowed.

And above all else, I ask that every degree of knowledge achieved may bring my child to a greater closeness to you and to a more abundant share of your love.

FOR A CHILD'S SOCIAL LIFE

Dear Jesus, you blessed the fun and merriment of the marriage of Cana, and you made the world a pleasant place to live in. My child is growing to a greater independence now in his [her] social life and goes with self-chosen companions — goes to dances and movies, to parties and social gatherings — as do all young people. This is natural, and you will give your blessings in all those pleasures if they are taken and enjoyed according to your wishes. Give judgment to my child in the choice of companions and activities and give judgment to me in the parental counsel I must exercise to guide him [her]. Bless my child — who is much more your child — and keep all his [her] pleasures clean and wholesome and such that they may always be offered up to you.

FOR A CHILD'S WISE CHOICE OF COMPANIONS

Dear Mother Mary, my child is beginning to move away from my complete supervision, and that is natural. It will mean so much for him [her] to have wholesome, good companions, boys and girls. From now on I must, of necessity, leave much to his [her] choice, though I also know that I must keep a watchful, loving care. You realize — better than I do — how precious my child's soul is and how bad companions can ruin it. So, with me, dear Mother, ask your Son, who once was young, too, to guide my son [daughter] in the choice of each and every friend.

FOR A CHILD'S VOCATION

Dear Lord Jesus, you have entrusted this child to my keeping. He [she] is growing older now and must soon decide upon a future state of life. Please help him [her] and help me to help my child to make the decisions you want. I would be very proud and happy if you called him [her] to make a complete consecration of his [her] life to you, but you know what is best. Whatever are your designs, just let my child know them, and grant the needed grace to follow them.

FOR A WISE CHOICE
OF A MARRIAGE PARTNER

Dear Mother Mary, I, a mother, come to you to ask you to guide my boy

[girl] in the choice of a life-companion. Don't let my child be carried away by false charms or be fascinated by mere outward glamour, but guide his [her] mind to look beneath and beyond all external attractiveness for the deep qualities that are worthwhile. Above all, lead him [her] to find a partner who is a good person and fervent Catholic, true in thought and word and deed to those ideals which are yours. Mother Mary, help another mother's child, who is yours, too. I will be letting him [her] go soon, but please don't ever let my child go from you.

FOR A SON OR DAUGHTER WHO IS ENGAGED

Mother Mary, my son [daughter] seems to have found the companion he [she] wants to marry. I hope the choice is well made and that your Son and you approve. Let these two young ones grow in mutual understanding and love, and let them learn to put up with each other's faults and frailties. Keep their love unsullied during their time of courtship, so that when they kneel at the altar our Lord will be fully pleased with them and bless them much. Mother of Fair Love, watch over them and keep them yours.

FOR A MARRIED SON OR DAUGHTER

Lord God, you yourself instituted marriage in the beginning and, when you became man upon earth, made it a sacrament. Watch over my son and his wife [my daughter and her husband] and give them grace to grow in love for each other and to become "one in mind, one in heart, and one in affection." Teach them how to help each other to carry the burdens of life in a saintly way and to walk joyfully and holily together through all the years to come. Let each be to the other, unto the very end, "a keepsake for heaven."

FOR A SON IN THE PRIESTHOOD OR STUDYING FOR THE PRIESTHOOD

Lord Jesus, eternal priest, bestow on my son a fullness of your perfection and strength. Remember that he has forsaken all things to give himself entirely to you. In his hours of loneliness and discouragement be close to him, that he may not fail in his sacred duties. Bless his labors with abundant fruit for souls. May all his contacts with others bring them and him closer to your most Sacred Heart.

Give him a sympathetic and understanding heart that he may restore peace and bring consolation to those who have fallen into sin. Give him a generous heart that he may share the sorrows and sufferings of others and be forgetful of his own. Give him a strong heart that he may be ever pure in the midst of a sinful world. Keep always holy his anointed hands, which are privileged to touch your sacred Body, that they may never work to your dishonor. May his lips, which touch your precious Blood, never be the instrument of sin.

And if ever, Lord, through weakness he should fail, then lift him gently in your Sacred Heart. Remember that the world's possessions are no longer his and that he has nothing left but you. Grant that each precious host to be consecrated at his hands may bring him closer to you.

Jesus, meek and humble of heart, Make his heart like unto your very own!

FOR A SON OR DAUGHTER IN RELIGIOUS LIFE

Lord Jesus, through an act of gracious love and mercy, you have called my son [daughter] to an intimate consecration to you. I thank you with all my heart for the precious grace thus bestowed upon my child, upon me, and upon our family.

But I realize, Lord, that in this consecration of my child human weakness remains. The gift of the soul thus generously offered is carried in a fragile body. Grant that he [she] may be ever free from sin.

May he [she] remain close to you throughout life in all things — and thus in every contact with others be an effective means to bring them, too, close to you through love and example.

May his [her] work be fruitful, and may the souls brought to you become for him [her] a source of encouragement in this life and eternal glory in the next.

May peace and joy ever attend my child in the consolations of your love.

LITANY OF
OUR MOTHER OF MOTHERS

Lord, have mercy on us.
> *Christ, have mercy on us.*
Lord, have mercy on us. Christ, hear us.
> *Christ, graciously hear us.*
God the Father of heaven,
> *have mercy on us.*
God the Son, redeemer of the world,
God the Holy Spirit,
Holy Trinity, one God,

Holy Mary,   *pray for us.*
Chaste daughter of the Father,
Chaste spouse of the Holy Spirit,
Chaste mother of the Son of God,
Vessel of election,
Throne of the divine Majesty,
Tabernacle of the divine Word,
Chalice of the divine life,

NUESTRA SEÑORA DE LA LECHE

Our Nursing Mother of Happy Delivery
La Leche Shrine. St Augustine, Florida.

Mother of God,   *pray for us.*
Mother of the infant Christ,
Consecration of womanhood,
Hope of Christian womanhood,
Model of Christian womanhood,
Blessed in your motherhood,
Inspiration of holy motherhood,
Consolation of motherhood,
Protector of motherhood,
Blessing of all Christian
    motherhood,
Exaltation of motherhood,
Sanctification of motherhood,
Queen of the most holy family,
Queen of chaste family life,
Queen of mothers,
Mother of mothers,
Mother of happy delivery,
Lamb of God, who take away the
    sins of the world,

                    spare us, Lord.

Lamb of God, who take away the sins of the world,

> *graciously hear us, Lord*.

Lamb of God, who take away the sins of the world,

> *have mercy on us*.

℣. Our Lady of Happy Delivery,

℞. Pray for us, who have recourse to you.

Let us pray:

Cherished Virgin, heaven's queen, chosen before all women to be the mother of the Son of God, Mary, my mother, who in your maternity so sanctified the state of holy motherhood, imploringly I come to you; humbly I beseech you; confidently I trust in you. I know that, by your powerful intercession, you can help me in my need. In you I take refuge, dear virgin. Poor and needy, I turn devoutly to you and place all confidently in your hands. Accept my humble trust, hear my petitions, and come to my aid, dear Mother of mothers.

℣. Behold the handmaid of the Lord;
℟. Be it done to me according to your word!

NOVENA IN HONOR OF
OUR MOTHER OF MOTHERS

Ant. Who is she that comes forth as beautiful as the rising dawn — as fair as the moon, as bright as the sun, as awe-inspiring as bannered troops arrayed!

I am the Mother of Fair Love, and of peace, and of knowledge, and of holy hope.
In me there is grace of the way and of truth; in me there is hope of life and of virtue.
Come over to me, all you who desire my blessings, and be filled with graces that are mine.
For my spirit is sweeter than honey, and my gifts a delight beyond measure.

Mother of Mothers, Pray for us!
Our Mother of Mothers Shrine
North Riverside, Illinois.

My memory is unto everlasting generations.

They who receive of my graces shall hunger still; and they who drink of my wisdom shall thirst for more.

One who listens to me shall not be confounded; and those who work according to my ways shall not sin.

Those who explain me with love shall have life everlasting.

Ant. Who is she that comes forth as beautiful as the rising dawn — as fair as the moon, as bright as the sun, as awe-inspiring as bannered troops arrayed!

Let us pray:

Most tender and loving Mother Mary, in union with you I adore the God of love and wisdom, whose tender mercies are manifest in you, his masterpiece of grace. And, while joyfully giving thanks for these mercies, I turn to you with confidence and love, begging you to join your powerful intercession to my poor prayers in order to obtain the blessings of motherhood that I seek.

The responsibilities and needs of motherhood are great, and no mother knows this better than you. So confidently I look to you to obtain God's abundant blessings on every phase of my motherhood, now and always.

℣. Pray for us, holy Mother Mary,
℟. That we may be made worthy of the promises of Christ.

Let us pray:

Heavenly Father, you were pleased that at the message of an angel your Word should take flesh in the womb of the Blessed Virgin Mary. Grant that we who humbly pray to you, and who believe her to be truly the Mother of God, may be helped by the prayers she offers you on our behalf, through the same Jesus Christ, your Son our Lord, who lives and reigns with you in the unity of the Holy Spirit, God, throughout all ages.

℟. Amen.

℣. Mother of mothers,
℟. Pray for us!

For

Times

of

Special

Problems

MEMORARE

Remember, most gracious Virgin Mary, that never was it known that anyone who fled to your protection, implored your help, or sought your intercession was left unaided. Inspired with this confidence, I fly unto you, dear Virgin of Virgins, my mother; to you I come, before you I stand, sinful and sorrowful. Mother of the Word Incarnate, despise not my petitions, but in your mercy hear and answer me. Amen.

FOR EVERY NEED OF MOTHERHOOD

Cherished Virgin, heaven's queen, chosen before all women to be the mother of the Son of God, Mary, my mother, who in your maternity so

84

sanctified the state of holy motherhood, imploringly I come to you; humbly I beseech you; confidently I trust in you. I know that, by your powerful intercession, you can help me in my need. In you I take refuge, dear Virgin. Poor and needy, I turn devoutly to you and place all confidently in your hands. Accept my humble trust, hear my petitions, and come to my aid, dear Mother of Mothers.

Behold the handmaid of the Lord;
Be it done to me according to your word!

PETITIONS TO MARY

Mary, by your holy motherhood,
  Hear the prayer of a mother!
  You who clasped the infant Jesus
tenderly in your arms,

Protect my child.

You who anxiously searched for the boy Christ in the temple,

Be anxious about my concerns.

You who experienced loneliness during the public life of your Son,

Teach me to bear my loneliness with a cheerful and courageous spirit.

You whose heart was pierced with sorrow at the foot of the cross,

Obtain strength for me when troubles come.

You who dwell in heavenly glory as mother of the Son of God and as queen of mothers,

Help me to express love and joy in my life and be my secure protection and my hope. Amen.

MARY, HELP ME

Holy Queen, mother of mothers, consolation and protectress of all Christian motherhood, Mother Mary, help me.

In all the trials and sorrows that come into my day, dear Mary, help me.

When I am tired with my labors and despondency is upon me, dear Mary, help me.

When all looks dark and I find none to speak a consoling or cheering word, dear Mary, help me.

When I am wearied by the weight of countless vexing little things and my patience is sorely tried, dear Mary, help me.

In the impatience and rudeness of others, by the example of your mildness, dear Mary, help me.

When others speak sharply to me and I would speak harshly in return, that I may show the gentleness of your own kindly speech, dear Mary, help me.

When my efforts seem to bear so little fruit and to be so little appreciated and I am discouraged, dear Mary, help me.

When a thousand worrisome distractions and annoyances come into my day and it seems so hard to keep my peace of heart, dear Mary, help me.

When all others seem to fail, then especially with the sweet support of your gentle aid, dear Mary, help me.

In all things, Mother, assist me! That I may, like you, with patience turn all my trials into spiritual treasures; that I may grow ever more like you, the cherished queen of the most holy family, dear Mary, help me!

RESIGNATION

(mother of an infant lost at birth)

Mary, my mother, obtain for me, I beg you, the grace of a holy resignation. Obtain for me the grace to understand this trial which is so hard for me to bear. I know that God in his all-wise providence has seen that it is for the best. Yet it is hard for me to bear the grief I feel. I come to you, dear mother, comforter of the afflicted and constant aid of those who trust in you. I know that you can obtain for me the peace and resignation that I seek. I confide in you entirely in this my tribulation and sorrow. You know the meaning of a mother's love, and can understand the depth of my affliction. Be to me a tender and protecting mother. For now, dear Mother Mary, I feel more than ever the need of your motherly love and sweet consolation.

Mary sorrowing, Mother of all Christians,
Pray for us!

TO AN INFANT IN HEAVEN
(petition)

My darling [*mention the child's name*] you are now in joy in the presence of our God; and in your spotless innocence, which he loves, you can speak to him with a voice that he will heed.

You are still my little baby and will surely regard the prayers of your mother, who bore you. So with confidence, then, I speak to you. Intercede for me to obtain the favor that I here ask as a mother through her child who stands before the throne of God [*here mention petition*].

But, if what I ask is not according to the wisdom and loving designs of almighty God for me and others, then ask him to grant what is best according to his good pleasure and to give me the wisdom and faith to conform my will to his.

TO A CHILD IN HEAVEN

(resignation)

My darling, you have gone to heaven to be eternally happy, and are now in joy in the company of the holy innocents there. It was a thing hard for me to understand when you were taken from my arms, for parting with you has caused me grief that few can know. Yet in all my grief I am happy, very happy for you, because I know the joy that is yours. Your joy is now my joy, too, because I can always feel that I had a part in bringing it to you. Now that you are in heaven, I realize that you are mine in a truer sense than you could ever be on earth. I cannot lose you now through sin. While parting with you was hard, I would not wish you back because I know that you are happier than I could ever make you here with me.

Help me, as you now can with your intercession, that I may be completely faithful to all my duties here on earth and merit to receive you again in eternal joys where there will be no more sorrow or parting from those we love.

Most Sacred Heart of Jesus, lover of little children,
  Hear my prayer!

AFTER DIFFICULTIES
BROUGHT ON BY CHILDBIRTH

Most loving Jesus, I look with humble trust to your adorable heart that once beat with such tender love as you took the little children to yourself and blessed them.
Remember, Lord, that it was through allowing little children to come to you that I received this affliction. I do not regret the consequence

of sufferings that are mine. I willingly accept them all according to your holy will, if they are best for me.

However, I know, too, that you are omnipotent, since you are God. So I ask you, if it may be according to your most loving designs, to grant me the remedy for which I now hope and pray. And, if you should see fit to grant it, may I use my restored health ever to the attainment of your greater glory.

AT A DIFFICULT DELIVERY

(to be said by nurse or attendant)

Mary, you are known by the beautiful title of Mother of Happy Delivery. You have cherished this title, and you have obtained numerous favors for those who have invoked you by it, because the title has been pleasing to you.

So confidently we now come to you, aware that your power with God is great and that your heart beats with undying affection for your children who implore your aid. Speak to your divine Son with us, Mary, and beg him, the lover of little children, to show again the favor of his love and spare this mother and child.

Our Lady of Happy Delivery,
Pray for her!

FOR A MOTHER IN A CRITICAL CONDITION AFTER CHILDBIRTH

(to be said by nurse or attendant)

Mother Mary, we look to your loving heart and ask you to have regard for this mother. You are a mother and know the meaning of motherhood. You cared for your infant Son and you know the need of a child for a mother's care and a mother's love. In the name of your holy motherhood, then, we come to you. Your divine motherhood was your greatest privilege. Do not deny our petition now made under the invocation of this precious title.

Turn to your divine Son, Mary; and, if it is to his greater glory, beg him with us for the health of N. Remind him that her affliction came because she obeyed his command to allow little children to come to him. Lend your intercession and ask your divine Son to spare this mother for the little one she has presented to him according to his word, so that with her restored health she may, in gratitude and love, direct in his holy ways the soul of the child she has so generously given to him.

Health of the Sick,
Pray for her!

FOR A BEREAVED MOTHER

Mary, what can I say now that my child is gone? Mother of Sorrows, to you I turn for help and comfort. I have lost my child, just as you lost your son Jesus when you stood beneath the cross and saw him die for our sins. You suffered so much, Mary, and you must know what I am suffering. I do not understand why God has allowed this sorrow to come into my life; yet I know that he is my loving father and that he is all good. I must be patient and trustful. Heavenly Mother, pray that I may have strength.

What are those words, so gentle and consoling, I seem to hear you say? Yes, my child is happy in heaven, or will soon be in heaven. Some day we are going to meet again where there will be no more sadness, no more parting. Until then I will look to you holding your divine Son in your arms and I know you will help me to understand and bear my sorrow.

My Mother, my Trust!

AT THE DEATH OF A CHILD

Most sorrowful Mother, your only son was called the fairest of all the sons of men. And you lost your boy in death on Calvary.

"O all ye who pass by the way attend and see if there be any sorrow like unto my sorrow!"

Mary, my child is gone now, too — and in this earthly life I shall never see my dear one again. And still I would not have it otherwise because I know that God wished to take my darling away young and innocent, before this world had cast its shadow upon that precious soul. And I am grateful for the assurance that my child is safe with Jesus and close to you.

Yet, dear Mother, I must carry on here below.

Remind your divine Son of the emptiness that my mother's heart must now know in this loss, and ask with me that I may have the strength and comfort that I so greatly need.

May I in faith, like you, be humbly submissive to the end.

At the cross, your station keeping,
Mournful Mother, you stood weeping,
Close to Jesus to the last.

Mother of Love, of Sorrow, and of Mercy,
Pray for us!

FOR THE HEALTH OF A CHILD

Holy Mother, health of the sick and constant aid of those who pray to you, please speak with me to your divine Son. He showed himself loving and merciful in healing the afflictions of the body, as well as those of the soul. Pray with me, then, that my child may regain full health and bodily vigor; and, with strength restored through your assistance, may he [she] become more deeply aware of the goodness of

God and understand better your all-embracing motherhood — and so glorify God and honor you by holiness of life and service of others.

Mary, sorrowing, Mother of all Christians,
Pray for us!

FOR A SICK CHILD

Dearest Mother, how helpless I feel in the presence of my ailing child! No labor of my hands, or sacrifice of my energy, can restore it quickly to health. And yet my heart yearns to do something for my child.

So to you I turn, dear mother, consoler of the afflicted and health of the sick. Show your loving protection once more and, as my child was

blessed in my womb and at its birth,
so intercede for it now that God may
restore its health of body.

I renew the consecration of my
child to you forever, most cherished
mother. In sickness and in health
may it be always yours.

*Mary, sorrowing, Mother of all
Christians,*
Pray for us!

FOR A HANDICAPPED CHILD

My God, you have seen fit in the
depth of your wisdom that my child
should be denied abilities that
children normally have.

I know that, however hidden, there is
a wise providence behind this and
that this providence is good.

I know, too, that a child who is

less privileged is a special trust given to a mother and a father, requiring special patience and love.

So, as you have committed this trust to my husband, to me, and to our family, dear Lord, please give us the wisdom to know what to do properly for this child. Guide us that we may in all things do what is best and so act in accord with your gracious providence, which is always a providence of love.

FOR AN EMOTIONALLY DISTURBED CHILD

Loving Jesus, teach me the wisdom that must be mine in order to understand and assist my child.

Direct my thoughts that I may best perceive what is to be done.

Direct my speech that I may say the right and helpful things, that will win the affection and confidence of my child and draw us closer together, and that I may not say the things that will needlessly disturb.

Guide my actions in any correction or direction that I am required to give, that it may be given in a way that will be helpful, and not in a way that will ever harm.

Give me patience — a wise, courageous, firm patience — that will direct me to assist my child in meeting the events of life with proper judgment and acceptance; a tender patience, that will help me gently and realistically to assist my child in the fulfillment of your loving purposes in his [her] regard.

FOR A CHILD IN DANGER OF BODILY HARM

Mother Mary, you know I am powerless now to be with my child and to offer protection in dangers that threaten. And, even if I could be present, there is little I could do. But you can assist my child, and your gracious and well-merited title of Mother of Perpetual Help inspires me to confidence that your intercession will be a protection now. Do not be deaf to the pleading of a mother's heart. You are a mother, and you understand. Speak to Jesus with me, then, and I know that he will have regard for our prayers.

Mary, Mother of Perpetual Help,
Pray for us who have recourse to you!

FOR A CHILD
EXPOSED TO MORAL DANGER

Mother most pure, from your very conception you were guarded from the least stain of sin. Speak to your divine Son with me now for the protection of my child against dangers of soul.

You know how greatly sin offends God and you abhor it. You know, too, how horrible sin is because of all that your divine Son suffered on account of it. Ask him now to defend my child from all dangers of sin that threaten. Please ask him to grant the protection of his grace, so that grievous sin will not possess the soul of my child and prevent us from sharing happiness together in heaven!

Mother most holy,
Pray for us!

FOR A SICK HUSBAND

Most tender Jesus, when you walked the earth, you were known everywhere as the divine healer. In the Gospels we learn how the sick were brought to you in numbers by their friends and relatives and are told how, without exception, they received your compassion — when as many as were brought to you were healed of their infirmities.

Now as of old you are still the omnipotent physician, and the mercy of your Sacred Heart has not changed. With confidence, then, I turn to you now, that you might lay the hand of your healing mercy on my sick husband and restore him to health.

Most Sacred Heart of Jesus,
I place my trust in you!

FOR A WAYWARD SON

Holy Mother of Sorrows, you endured a most bitter agony for wayward children as you stood beside your crucified Son, and you know the dreadful tragedy of sin.

Now my son has gone astray in a life of sin. Have pity on him. I love him, Mother, because he is mine; I bore him and cared for him. I know that you love him dearly, too, because you suffered so much for his salvation.

Please, then, pray now to your Son with me: remind your Son how much my boy means to him and to you and to me. Mother, obtain guidance for my child that will lead him gently and surely back to the right way, and bring him to understand the power of your intercession and the love of your divine Son.

FOR A WAYWARD DAUGHTER

Holy Virgin Mary, you are the consecration and the protectress of all Christian womanhood. The glory of your own pure womanhood is dear to you and you wish to see its beauty reflected in all your daughters. Let the image of this womanhood then shine upon my precious daughter. May the grace of your divine Son touch her heart and awaken there a love for you and for the womanhood that is resplendent in you. May it guide her erring feet and bring her back to your Son in holiness of life.

Shelter her, Mary, beneath your protecting mantle and take her close in your motherly embrace. Remember that she is your child as well as mine and needs your protection as her mother, more than the many who have not strayed. To you, Mother, I commend her; speak to your Son with me for her restoration to a holy and virtuous life.

Mary, our Hope,
Have pity on us!

FOR A DECEASED HUSBAND

Long ago, dear Lord, you reminded us that our ways are not your ways, that your thoughts are not our thoughts.

It is difficult at times to understand your ways, your providence. But by faith we are assured that your providence is always a providence of love. I look to you now, the resurrection and the life, and I am reminded of those consoling words — that "for your faithful life is *changed,* not taken away" ... and that, "when the abode of this earthly life is dissolved, an eternal dwelling is prepared for us."

It is filled with an assured faith in these promises that I come to you and pray in my grief for my deceased husband. Take him in your mercy into the company of your saints. Mercifully grant him that rest and joy which is the reward of

fidelity in all our earthly struggles.
And grant that one day I may join
him in happiness in your eternal
dwellings where death shall no more
separate us.

Eternal rest grant unto him, Lord,
And let perpetual light shine upon
him!

FOR A WIDOWED MOTHER

Mary, I know you understand. And
because you so understand the
sorrows and trials that are mine,
I ask your comfort and help. A
mother's burden is not an easy one.
But now I find myself not only with
a mother's work, but with the responsibilities of a father as well.
And together with this I am denied
the comfort and consolation of a

husband, who is lost to me until we shall be reunited in heaven.

In my troubles, then, I come to you, dear mother. You were a widow, too, and knew the terrible aloneness when Joseph left this earth and Jesus departed from your home. By all that you then suffered in your immaculate heart, I beg you to assist me with the comfort and strength that your understanding and motherly intercession may offer me. Be close to me, Mary, for now I need your comfort and help more than ever before.

Comforter of the Afflicted,
Pray for us!

IN EVERY AFFLICTION

Immaculate Virgin Mary, your place

in the heart of your divine Son proclaims you the protecting mother and constant aid of afflicted children.

With utmost confidence, then, I come to you and beg you to speak to your Son with me in my sorrow. You are the mother of sorrows and the queen of martyrs, and thus you know well the depth of our suffering and misery. You are the mother of us all, and thus you are solicitous for your children in every affliction. And, more than this, you are powerful to help us in our wretchedness and want; for you are the mother of God, and he will not deny you your requests.

Confidently, then, I trust in you, dear mother, in this my misery and affliction. Be to me a protecting

mother, and I know your Son will
grant me the strength and peace for
which I pray.

Immaculate Queen of Peace,
Pray for us!

FOR GRACE TO OVERCOME SOME PERSONAL PROBLEM OR WEAKNESS

(especially suited to alcoholics)

Lord Jesus Christ, you are the
strength of the weak and the
confidence of those who trust in you.
Be my secure confidence and my
abundant strength!
Teach me to understand myself
and to believe in the effectiveness
of your saving grace. Grant me the
courage not to stop trying and teach
me the humility to trust in you when

I tend to be discouraged by my weakness.

Give me, too, the honesty needed to face my problem without excuse and without pretense, and give me the practical good sense to accept the means needed to help myself.

Toward any who may criticize me, give me charity; with those who do not understand, give me patience; and give me the humility to accept whatever aid I may receive from those who want to help me.

And, above all, let me never forget that you love me and that you earnestly want to help me. Let me be completely convinced, too, that you more than anyone *can* assist me — and that you will support me at all times if only I learn to put a realistic trust in you.

Blessings

and

Feasts

BLESSINGS BY A PRIEST

Blessings that the Church has ordained for certain special occasions are known as sacramentals. In the *Constitution on the Sacred Liturgy*, the Second Vatican Council tells us:

"These are sacred signs which are patterned after the sacraments. They clearly signify certain spiritual effects which are obtained through the intercession of the Church. By means of them we may be disposed to receive the principal benefits produced by the sacraments and thus the various occasions of our life are rendered holy.

"Consequently, the liturgy of the sacraments and of the sacramentals brings it about that, for those of the faithful who are properly disposed, practically every aspect of life is made holy by the divinely given grace flowing from the paschal mystery of the passion, death, and resurrection of Christ — from which source all the sacraments and sacramentals derive their worth; and there is practically no proper use of material things that cannot be directed to the holiness of man and the praise of God.''

There are certain of the sacramental blessings which, on occasions, may be of very special meaning for mothers. Some explanation follows, which may help to a better understanding. For, as Vatican Council II reminds us, through them ''various occasions of our life are rendered holy.''

FOR AN EXPECTANT MOTHER

The Church, mindful of the sacredness of a mother's office and aware of the difficulties and dangers that frequently attend it, has wisely decreed a special blessing for expectant mothers.

It would seem good if more mothers sought this blessing.

The blessing may be received either at home or at the church.

Prayers taken from the blessing follow:

Lord God, creator of all things, strong and mighty, just and merciful, you alone are all good and kind. You delivered Israel from all evil, making our fathers pleasing in your sight; and you sanctified them by the hand of your Holy Spirit. You prepared the body and soul of the glorious Virgin Mary, by the cooperation of the Holy Spirit, in order that she might be a worthy dwelling for your Son. You filled John the Baptist with the Holy Spirit and made him rejoice in his mother's womb. So now receive the sacrifice of a contrite heart and the fervent desire of this devoted mother, N , who humbly asks you for the preservation of her child, which you have helped her to conceive. Guard her and defend her from all deceit and hurt of the wicked enemy so that, by the birthgiving hand of your mercy, her child may come happily to the light of regeneration and deserve to be joined to you in all things and merit to gain eternal life, through the same Jesus Christ our Lord, your Son, who lives and reigns with you in the unity of the same Spirit. Amen.

Let us Pray.

Come, we beg you, Lord, to this dwelling, and drive all danger far from it and from this your devoted servant, N . Let your holy angels dwell here, and let them keep her and her child in peace; and let your blessing be always with her. Save them, almighty God, and grant to them your perpetual light, through Christ our Lord.

R̷. Amen.

Finally, as the priest makes the sign of the cross over the mother, he says:

May the blessing of almighty God, of the Father and of the Son and of the Holy Spirit, descend upon you, and upon your child, and remain with you forever.

R⁷. Amen.

AFTER CHILDBIRTH

Motherhood is a sacred thing. When a mother has borne a child, she has fulfilled a sublime and holy role. The little child which she treasures is likewise very precious in the eyes of God. Rightly, then, the Church has ordained that the mother and child should receive its special blessing.

On the occasion of this blessing,

the mother comes to offer thanks for the favor granted her in her maternity, and to ask protection and grace in her office of motherhood.

The priest can give this special blessing. Catholic mothers, in their solicitude for the welfare of their children and in their desire to fulfill properly their office of directing them through life, should anxiously seek the benefits that such a blessing can bring.

The mother may come alone, or (a more laudable thing) she may bring her child, or children, when the blessing is received.

The ceremony begins at the entrance of the church. Here a brief exhortation may be delivered to the mother (who holds a lighted candle) and to any others who accompany her.

Mary, Confidence of Christian Motherhood,
Be my help and my protection.

Then the priest addresses all:

Peace be with you !

After this the priest leads the mother and the others into the church towards the altar, saying to the mother:

Enter the temple of God; adore the Son of the Blessed Virgin Mary, who has given you the blessing of motherhood.

At the altar, the mother places her candle in a candlestick, and all (standing) recite the Magnificat:

My soul magnifies the Lord, and my spirit rejoices in God my savior, because he has regarded the lowliness of his handmaid. For, behold, henceforth all generations shall call me blessed, because he who is mighty has done great things for me, and holy is his name. And his mercy is from generation to generation on those who fear him. He has shown might with his arm; he has scattered the proud in the conceit of their heart. He has put down the mighty from their thrones, and has exalted the lowly. He has filled the hungry with good things, and the rich he has sent away empty. He has given help to Israel, his servant, mindful of his mercy — even as he spoke to our fathers — to Abraham and to his posterity forever.*

Then all kneel as the priest continues with the people:

℣. Lord, have mercy.

℟. Christ, have mercy.

℣. Lord, have mercy.

℟. Our father [*silently as far as:*]

*Confraternity version, with permission.

℣. And lead us not into temptation.

℟. But deliver us from evil.

℣. Lord, hear my prayer.

℟. And let my cry come to you.

℣. The Lord be with you.

℟. And with your spirit.

Then the priest:

Let us pray. Almighty, everlasting God, through the childbearing of the Blessed Virgin Mary, you have turned the pains of the faithful at childbirth into joy. Look now with your love upon this devoted mother who joyfully comes to your holy temple to offer thanks; and grant that after this life, through the merits and intercession of the same Blessed Virgin Mary, she and her child may deserve to be admitted to

eternal joy, through Christ our Lord.
R̷. Amen.

*If the mother has brought the child,
the priest may bless the child as
follows:*

Let us pray. Lord Jesus Christ,
son of the living God, though you
were begotten before all ages, you
wished in time to become an infant,
and you love the innocence of childhood. And, when the little ones
were brought to you, you tenderly
embraced them and blessed them.
So now protect this infant with the
blessings of your affection, so that
the forces of evil may not harm its
soul. Grant that, advancing in age
and wisdom and grace, it may ever
be pleasing to you, who live and
reign with God the Father, in the

unity of the Holy Spirit, God forever.

R̷. Amen.

Then the priest blesses the mother and child, sprinkling them with holy water, saying:

May the peace and blessing of God almighty, the Father and the Son and the Holy Spirit, descend upon you and remain forever.

R̷. Amen.

FOR A CHILD

Apart from the blessing for an infant which is conferred on the occasion of the blessing of a mother after child-birth (p. 125), the Church also has a blessing for older children. A prayer taken from this blessing is given here:

Lord Jesus Christ, son of the living God, who said, "Permit the little children to come to me, and forbid them not, for the kingdom of heaven is for such," pour the graces of your blessing upon this your child, and be mindful of the faith and devotion of the Church and of its parents; so that, growing in virtue and wisdom before God and men, this child may attain a blessed old age and enjoy eternal salvation, you who live and reign forever.

℟. Amen.

OTHER BLESSINGS

There are additional blessings which may have a profound meaning for members of the family, and which, on occasions, may be profitably sought.

1. Blessing after childbirth of a mother who has lost her baby.

This blessing may be comforting, indeed, to a mother who knows the sorrow of being deprived of her little one. Through it, graces to understand God's providence in her loss, and greater help to bear up under her sorrow, may be her assured hope.

2. Blessing for sick children who are too young to receive the sacrament of anointing of the sick.

It would be wise for mothers to seek this blessing in any greater sickness, and not wait until there is extreme danger for the welfare of the child.

3. Blessing for a sick adult.

The sacrament of anointing of the sick is, of course, administered in times of grave danger. But there is also this blessing in a lesser sickness, which, if convenient, might well be sought.

4. Blessing of a home.

It is a beautiful custom of Catholics to ask God's blessing on their home and on those who dwell in it. Such a blessing would be wisely sought by all Catholic families.

FEASTS OF MARY HONORING MOTHERHOOD

The motherhood of Mary is a glory not only for herself but for all womanhood. The Church never tires of singing the praises of this motherhood in the Masses for Mary's feasts. Some of the feasts more especially pertinent to her maternity are listed here. It would be well for Catholic

*mothers to make themselves familiar
with the meanings of these feasts and
endeavor to enter into the spirit of
them as occasion may offer.*

THE ANNUNCIATION (March 25) This
is the great feast of our Lady's
maternity. It commemorates that
holy moment when the Angel Gabriel brought the glad news to Mary
that she had been chosen to be the
mother of God, and when, as St.
John tells us, "the Word was made
flesh" in her virginal womb.

THE VISITATION (July 2) On the occasion of the Annunciation the
Angel Gabriel told our Lady that her
cousin Elizabeth was also with
child. Elizabeth was old; so Mary —
now an expectant mother, too —

went to help her cousin until the time of delivery. Here Mary, even during her lifetime on earth, was manifesting that sweet solicitude for expectant mothers which has won for her the endearing titles of Mother of Mothers and Our Lady of Happy Delivery.

THE MATERNITY (October 11) The divine maternity is the greatest prerogative of our Lady. Through it she has been raised to a dignity accorded to no other purely human being. Through it, too, the motherhood of all future women was elevated to a glory never known before. It is fitting, then, that this maternity should be honored with a special feast.

THE EXPECTATION (December 18) This former feast of Mary is no longer listed for *liturgical* celebrations, though it still seems to have its attraction for mothers as a private devotion — inviting a week of prayerful togetherness with Mary as she warmly anticipates the coming of her infant on that first Christmas day.

Young mothers in their trials and perplexities may forget at times that our Lady was also an expectant mother. But she truly was. During the long months of waiting, how many times did Mary call up with the eyes of her imagination the face of her child, and picture it to herself by means of loving contemplation in a thousand different ways! Yes, Mary was an expectant mother; and she shares your time of expectation with loving concern. She is patroness of expectant mothers — Our Lady of Happy Delivery — and the Church in former times chose to honor her expectation by a special feast.

THE NATIVITY (December 25) While we rightly celebrate the feast of Christmas as the day on which our Savior was born, it is likewise in a very intimate way a commemoration of our Lady's maternity. If the joy of our Christmas has a peculiar warmth of meaning for us, this comes largely from the fact that God has come to us, not as a mighty judge, but as an infant, a companion partaking of our flesh and nature, born a little child of the virgin whose name was Mary.

THE PURIFICATION (February 2) Words from the Gospel of this feast explain: "They [his parents] carried Jesus to Jerusalem to present him to the Lord, as it is written in the law of the Lord." It was the Jewish custom to offer to God the first-born male child in this manner. The practice of this offering would seem to find something of a counterpart today in the beautiful practice of mothers who offer their children to God in a special way, prayerfully asking for them God's loving protection.

Councels

and

Helps

for

Wife

and

Mother

Infant Baptism in Emergency

DEATH WITHOUT BAPTISM

Since God gives us life in the Spirit and salvation through baptism, the loss of a baby before parents have had a chance to see to its baptism has been a cause of frequent anguish for those who desperately want their child to have a fulness of God's gifts.

These parents should know that the doctrine of a "limbo" as a place and state is not a firmly established teaching. Theologians have differed in their opinions about it, and the matter is still disputed. We do not know for certain the fate of unbaptised infants. Still, the obligation of parents to seek baptism

144

for their child is a grave one: it may not be taken lightly.

On the other hand when God takes a child before we have had a chance to secure the sacrament of baptism, there are comforting things we can and should tell ourselves about almighty God. For we know that God is a God of love. Jesus reminds us of the Father's work as a testimonial of this. We have only to look about us to see. And we perceive that the God of the universe in all its glory has given a tender thought to the smallest details—bringing a delicate beauty to the wild flowers, which are to fade tomorrow; feeding and caring for the little birds that are the work of his hands. And as for us? Will he not provide much more for you? Jesus asks. Why even the hairs of our head are counted, he tells us. We must learn to entrust much to his fatherly concern. We are in his hands. He can do all things. And he can have his own special ways of offering our little baby the joys of paradise. So we may well be comforted as we now entrust the child to the provision of a God whose providence is always a providence of love.

WHAT TO DO IN AN EMERGENCY The normal procedure for parents who want to do the right thing is for them to make arrangements for an early baptism of their child. For we know that it is through the scarament of baptism that we are form-

ed in the likeness of Christ and that
we are incorporated into the great
body of the faithful who constitute
the Church of Christ.

So it is important that infants at an
early time should receive this
incorporation; and, if there is
danger of death before a solemn
baptism may be properly arranged
and accomplished, then baptism
should be conferred privately by
someone qualified to do so.

This matter is of extreme importance.

When no Catholic is available, baptism for a Catholic child may be
performed by a person who is not
of the Catholic faith - or of any
Christian faith for that matter. To
do this, such a person need not
accept the Catholic Church or Christ-

ian beliefs, but is merely asked to do a great favor for the child, which its religion calls for and which the child cannot do for itself, in a situation where no one of the child's faith is available.

All that is requested in such circumstances is that the person involved: [1] want to do something for the child that is important and helpful according to the child's religion; [2] perform the action simply the way the child's Church prescribes; and [3] want for the child whatever good will come from performing the action properly.

Baptism is conferred by pouring water on the head of the one to be baptized and pronouncing *at the same time* the words: "I BAPTIZE YOU IN THE NAME OF THE FATHER, AND OF THE SON, AND OF THE HOLY SPIRIT."

In case of *premature* delivery the fetus, no matter at what stage of pregnancy, should be baptized unconditionally if life is certain; it should be baptized conditionally if life is doubtful.

Any motion on the part of the premature fetus may be taken as a sign of certain life. Lack of motion, however, is not a sure sign of death.

The formula for *conditional* baptism is: "*If you can be baptized*, I baptize you in the name of the Father, and of the Son, and of the Holy Spirit.''

If, when delivered, the fetus is enclosed in membranes, *these membranes should always be opened completely* so that baptism may be conferred directly on the premature child itself, not on the membranes.

For a fetus delivered in the early stages of pregnancy, baptism by immersion is a surer and better method.

The manner of administration by immersion is as follows: when the membrane has been broken, the fetus is completely immersed in water and withdrawn *while* the person who is baptizing pronounces the words of baptism.

If immersion in such cases is not immediately possible, rather than permit a dangerous delay, the water may be poured directly over the fetus that has been exposed by the opening of the membranes.

Mothers cannot be too well instructed in this matter of baptism. In the case of a miscarriage or in any danger of death for an unbaptized child, they should either endeavor to have the baptism performed by others or should perform it themselves.

Those who attend a pregnant woman in the time of an actual or imminent miscarriage should be on the alert to rescue the fetus and to perform the necessary baptism. At least conditional baptism should be given, even though there is no direct evidence of life whatever.

Explaining Life
to Children

WHAT AND WHEN

Mothers frequently ask, "What should I tell my little girl or boy about life? When should I speak of these matters? And how should I go about it?"

Probably no one who knows much about the matter would venture to set an age specification for such information. The answer to "when" is: Whenever the child begins showing curiosity about such matters.

Little Johnny, age five or six, may come to mother and ask where little babies come from. The question should not surprise or alarm; it should be answered. A wise mother will take a calm interest in the question, draw her child to her in a motherly fashion, and explain that God sends the little baby to parents. Little babies come from God.

Such an answer may satisfy entirely. Johnny's curiosity may be very much of the type of child curiosity that we see concerned about Santa Claus and the like. At first, it probably is that kind of curiosity. We should not magnify it beyond what it really is.

However, the child may want to know more. It may even be that he has heard something from an older child and has come to mother for the proper account. In this case, a mother should thank God for the child's confidence that has brought him to her for an explanation. Keep the confidence of the child.

If the child persists in a way that seems to make further explanation advisable, the mother may simply explain that when God gives the baby, it is very small; and so he puts it inside the mother's body, near her heart. God keeps it there for a while; and, when it is big enough (still a tiny baby), He brings it into the world for the mother to take care of.

Such an explanation, simply, sympathetically given, may satisfy the further curiosity of the child. If, however, the child's curiosity has been stimulated to the extent that he has asked this much, it is quite possible that he will press a further question. He may ask *how* God brings the baby into the world. If he asks this, a mother should again be deeply grateful that he has come to get the information from her and has not picked it up elsewhere.

But here, too, the mother need not magnify the question beyond the scope it actually has in the child's wondering mind. Perhaps one of the best things she may do in this case is to accept the child's ability to wonder at things and build on this. She may simply say that God is able to do things like this. God is all-powerful: He can do all things. He can make the soul of a little baby and cause a body to grow inside the mother. He can bring the little baby into the world: a thing like that isn't hard for God.

Simply and quietly this explanation may be given.

Isn't God wonderful! The child will possibly be thinking such thoughts of God himself. The mother will do well to suggest them. She might remind him to thank God often for making him. The wonderful God did this because he loved him.

A similar explanation, of course, could be given to a little girl. The time? When the child's curiosity seems to demand it.

A simple, delicate, factual explanation, such as the one suggested above, all hangs together. The child will never find out anything to the contrary, for the explanation is true.

Babies are in the hospital when they are very young because they are extremely delicate then and need special care. Mother, too, is in the hospital then because she is rather weak. While the baby was in her body, mother fed it with the food she ate.

Caring for the baby thus makes her a little weak. Then, too, mother should be near her baby while it is in the hospital. She wants to be near it. She feeds it at that time with her milk. After they leave the hospital, mother often takes the baby back to the doctor when it is still very young.

All this is *true* and will probably satisfy the child. To tell a child that storks or doctors bring babies is to give an explanation that deceives. The child may hear things to the contrary and suspect that there is something about the matter that mother is hiding, that mother doesn't want to tell. Child curiosity may then prompt the little one to try to learn the truth elsewhere. This may produce warped ideas on the matter, and much harm may be done.

Perhaps one of the greatest harms is that the child may lose confidence in his mother. If everything that the mother tells proves true, however, and she sympathetically and prudently answers the child's questions, the child will tend to come back when further curiosity is awakened.

Such a tendency to come to mother should be fostered. The child's confidence in her is above all to be preserved.

All this instruction has concerned itself with a possible very early inquiry of a child — inquiry which may catch a mother off guard if she does not prepare for it. There is the further problem, though, of the child who *does not* ask questions and still should have matters explained at a suitable age by his mother or father.

There is also the question of explaining the part the father plays in bringing new life into the world. A child must come by all this knowledge sooner or later, and the proper place to acquire it is in the home — and from the parents. The whole explanation may and should be given beautifully and reverently in a way that will inspire confidence in parents and will tend later on to beget purity in the child during the adolescent period. Space does not permit further instruction on the matter here, but parents would do well to anticipate such a need and to consult one or more of the better books or pamphlets that explain this matter.

(See also p. 51, prayer
For the Confidence of a Child)

Child Correction

Proper correction of a child is a great responsibility on the part of a parent. A child's character must be guided to maturity gently, but firmly, by the proper discipline. And this formation of the child's character begins in his earliest days.

Obedience is a great virtue of childhood. Of the Christ Child we are told: "He was subject to them [Mary and Joseph]." Obedience should be insisted on, and respect for parents in their proper exercise of authority should be demanded. But this respect will hardly be fostered unless the parents merit it by their conduct.

A parent should not allow a child to answer back in rebellion. Nor should a child be permitted to *argue* about obeying a command once the command has been explained and understood. A command that is not reasonable should not be given in the first place. And, once a reasonable command has been given, obedience should be insisted on calmly, with love, and with firmness.

Neither commands nor corrections should ever be given with a show of anger or with shouting that shows irritation. It is always a mistake to correct a child in a hasty manner or with a show of temper or anger. It is even more a mistake to strike a child in a fit of anger.

Corporal punishment may be necessary — in serious matters. But corporal punishment that does not ultimately foster love has been poorly administered. When a child is deliberately disobedient or insubordinate, that child is showing pride and is placing himself above the parent. Corporal punishment as a corrective reverses the process: it tends to establish the proper humility as a corrective to pride and places the child in the definite and proper place of subordination.

If corporal punishment is administered in anger, the child may recognize only the anger, not the reason for punishment. He may only be antagonized and may not profit. But, if the correction is administered with the proper calm and dignity (as all correction should be administered), the child will be far more likely to respond; for he may then realize he has done wrong but is still loved.

Above all, a parent should learn to pray for light and guidance in the office of child correction. Hasty words cannot be unsaid, and hasty actions cannot be undone. A moment of deliberation and prayer often makes the difference between a hasty and futile correction and a well-administered and profitable one.

(See also p. 53, prayer For Grace to Correct a Child Properly)

The Exceptional Child

Experience testifies that a small percentage of children born each year will be exceptional children, in need of some form of specialized help. A smaller percentage of these children will need institutional training away from home.

Now, no mother normally anticipates that *her* child will be one of these exceptional children. It is usually true that a mother will not tend to think of her child-to-be-born as one who might need to be released by her to another home for some special institutional help or training which she cannot give. Nor *should* she dwell upon such thoughts. The situation is relatively rare, but we must recognize that, however unlikely, the possibility is real.

In case there is an early evidence that a baby is an exceptional child, possibly in need of very special help, the awareness normally comes to a mother and a father with something of a shock. The situation was not expected, and the parents may experience something of a stunned perplexity about what they should do, how they should think in the situation that confronts them. It is important that their thinking and acting should be properly directed. Their Christian faith may teach them acceptance, but it still may leave them without practical guidelines that they should have at this time. And it is hoped that the following thoughts may be of benefit.

First of all, a mother must never, under any circumstances, tell herself that having such a child is a punishment sent to her by almighty God. It is not a punishment. God's providence may be hidden from human eyes; but this child, like any other, is a gift of his love. And, whatever the condition, it may bring as much love into the family as any other child.

A mother may be advised before she leaves the hospital that the child needs special care in a home for exceptional children. She may be advised to relinquish it to such special care and not take the baby home with her. This advice may be good. But, on the other hand, such advice may not always be wisely given —

even by those whose position would suggest a proper knowledge. Experience suggests that advice of this type is sometimes too hastily pressed upon a mother. In a doubtful situation, perhaps a solid initial counsel is this: if you *can* properly care for the baby at home, *wait and see*. Take the baby home and make the decision as facts and honest, mature consideration manifest the better way.

A mother may sometimes falsely tell herself, "God has given me this baby and perhaps He means for me to take care of it." This is not always true. At times a baby needs the specialized care that its mother cannot give and will need to be placed in a special home.

If you are reliably informed that you have an exceptional child, you must quietly and prayerfully face the facts. It can do you and your family mental and emotional harm to fight the facts by vainly going to doctor after doctor in search of one to tell you your child is not exceptional. The important thing is to discover the extent of your child's needs and to provide the most meaningful help.

It is sometimes said that the longer you wait to relinquish a child whom you must surrender, the harder it will be. This is not necessarily true. It may conceivably be easier after you have completely adjusted to the place of your selection.

It is argued that a retarded child will

warp the personalities of the other children. But it can be important for the other children's sake that they get to know the child. Such a child can do a lot for them. Knowing the child, at least for a while, they do not wonder about this little brother or sister of theirs who is somewhere else. There is no mystery about it. It is amazing how they can come to love such a baby — and frequent visits to such a child later away from home can then be good.

If you bring an exceptional child home with you, do not come home crying to the other children. Come home the way you came home with all the others. Let the children hold it. If they remark how small it is, give a happy smile and agree with them and say, "Isn't it sweet!"

Don't even start out by explaining that anything is wrong. In a sense it may seem very much to you as if you are playing a game in this. But this can have its advantages; the more normally your children act, the easier it is on you. The other children may be made aware of the exceptional condition over the weeks and months — or years — as occasion warrants. By all means, do not establish a tragedy: you will have to live with it if you do.

An exceptional child is *exceptional*. You must accept the child as it is. It is probably a very wise thing not to make comparisons of the development of *this* child with the development of your other children. Receive the exceptional child in terms of its own proper development. If you give such a baby half a chance, you may find that it is even more charming than your other children. Accept your baby for what it is and make the most of it. Don't try to act as if this child were the same as your other children: you must remember that this one is *exceptional*.

There is something, too, to remember about yourself. Not only is the child's situation exceptional, but *your* situation is exceptional as well. No matter how much counsel or how much help may be offered you, adjustment to the situation of an exceptional child may be slow to come. To know this is in itself a help towards a calmer and more realistic adjustment. Time, prayer, and patience will be required.

It may be the part of wisdom, too, for a mother to realize that the attitude she adopts can influence what people say to her. If she acts frantic about her situation, it may be natural enough for others to agree that her problems are too great to cope with. If she goes about making a cheerful effort that manifests acceptance, others may readily accept the situation with her and provide encouragement that may be helpful. We should know that at all times it is largely possible to create our own atmosphere for success or defeat in dealing with the exceptional situation that is ours.

If a child is entrusted to an institutional home, parents should want to take the child home occasionally. If this is not possible, they should want to visit the child. They should want to know and love him as one of the family, and have the child know and love them.

Many retarded children are decidedly educable, and under the proper patient and expert help they may develop to the extent of gainful employment in work suited to their abilities. Time may be needed to tell if they are capable of such development.

It is a lamentable situation, indeed, when parents do not accept a retarded child with their whole love. The retarded child feels it. It has been said that such children have a keener feeling on this point than others. They look for love, crave it. They are pleased with praise. Perhaps they can't do much, and they may be slow to learn; but, when you give them praise for what they succeed in doing, they respond eagerly. It can hardly be too highly stressed that patience and heartfelt love are the all-important tools in the education of the retarded child.

God's providence in our regard may at times be a bit difficult to comprehend. But one thing we must know: his providence is always a providence of love. And there is another thing that should not escape us: when God entrusts parents with an exceptional child, he is giving them something very special — a trust that is very dear to him. He commits to them a delicate task of patience and understanding, and invites them to undertake a special work of love. We should not miss this. And, if we turn to him confidently for guidance to fulfill that trust, we shall be able to understand, as only he may teach us, some of the finest secrets of his wisdom and love.

(*See also p. 104, prayer* For a Handicapped Child)

Breastfeeding

A baby comes into the world at the mercy of adults. And the adult world of our day has failed the generation of those being born in all too many ways. One of these ways, surely, has found its expression in the de-education of mothers in the area of breastfeeding and in the consequent deprivation of both mother and child of benefits and privileges that should be theirs.

Some doctors may discourage breastfeeding at times because it is more convenient not to be bothered with the occasional problems of a nursing mother — or possibly because in certain situations they may simply not be informed. Hospitals may sometimes discourage it because they are structured to patterns and timetables with which breastfeeding may conflict. Nurses may discourage it, following a harmonious course with the doctor and the hospital. Added to this, relatives and neighbors, well-meaning perhaps but uninformed, may discourage it because they claim it is old fashioned; and, with high self-approval, they may look with an ill-disguised sense of pity on the mother whose common sense has told her that breastfeeding is the better thing.

So it is no wonder if a young mother may be confused and discouraged from the outset.

But we know that almighty God has

planned breastfeeding for both mother and child as a part of his scheme of love. For best development, the baby needs such a secure relationship with its mother as breastfeeding provides. The mother needs this relationship, too, for proper fulfillment and for the realization of the proper bond of love with her child. It is part of God's plan. The way God planned it was to give a mother milk along with the baby. It is a very normal, correct thing for her to give this milk to her baby as its best food.

Mothers can do themselves and their baby a real disservice by wilfully neglecting this loving role of breastfeeding.

And mothers who care will be glad

to know of a wonderful source of needed practical help. It is the La Leche League International. This is a league of dedicated mothers who strongly advocate breastfeeding and who are actively helping other mothers who need encouragement or possibly instruction. And any mother who is interested in being better informed or in obtaining help in the area of breastfeeding is strongly encouraged to seek the assistance she may obtain through this nonsectarian, nonprofit organization. Address: La Leche League, International, Franklin Park, Illinois 60131. Such a mother may be especially interested in reading the assuring, beautifully-written book published by the La Leche League, *The Womanly Art of Breastfeeding.*

It is the League manual, and in most cases a reading of this book may perhaps constitute the best beginning point for a more informed thinking.

Forgiveness

Christ instituted the sacrament of his forgiveness to take away sin. He instituted it to effect reconciliation, to restore unity, to bring us peace of mind and heart. In a certain sense it seems that in this sacrament, perhaps more than anywhere else today, Christ offers us a direct revelation of his heart and of his abiding love. Surely it would be a pity for any of us to miss the fuller meanings of this sacrament.

If we do find difficulties in understanding, then it is just possible that we do not recognize sufficiently the meaningful relationship that exists with Christ and the fellowship of the faithful in this sacrament. All sin, whether we think of it this way or not, is somehow a setting of ourselves against God, and is an insubordination in which we prefer our will and our way to the will and wisdom of almighty God. Sin is a rebellious, treasonous act in which we place ourselves in opposition to Christ and to his kingdom.

To remedy this, we have the sacrament of Christ's forgiveness — a sacrament of reconciliation. On our part this sacrament is an explicit retraction of the position taken by our wayward will and actions, and an expression of loving sorrow; and, in response to our sorrow, the loving forgiveness of Christ restores us to our proper place in his heart and in his Church.

Sin offends God. This we know. But it also offends against the community of the faithful. Sometimes an aspect of this offense against my neighbor is obvious — as in the case of detraction, where I damage the reputation of another; in an insult, in theft, or in murder, where the damage is quite apparent.

Sin is a personal act. It is something for which I, in my waywardness, am responsible. But it is more: it is an act in me supported by the sinfulness, the waywardness, of the society in which I live. We see this factor at work in families. If parents are selfish and dishonest, we are not surprised that their children tend to become the same. Sin works very much like a contagion: it will be normal enough in such a family for the environment to foster tendencies of selfishness and greatly lessen the development of true love. So it is to a degree with my sin in relationship to my environment. This fact does not destroy guilt (perhaps even very grave guilt) on my part. But it may help to explain something that I should not miss. My sin is rendered easier by the sin of others.

The application that follows upon this seems fairly obvious: *my* sin is not merely an offense against God. It is an offense against my neighbor, against the Church, the body of Christ, as well. Because of my sin, the holiness of the society is to some degree lowered — and this sinfulness affecting the whole community renders me a debtor, in need of making up somehow to the body of the faithful as well as to God. Every sin is an offense against the love of God. It is also an offense against love of my neighbor.

In my sin and in my acts of virtue, I am never entirely alone: the acts are never restricted exclusively to a relationship with God in what I do, or even in what I merely think. We have been told by Christ to love one another as he has loved us. My virtuous act (though hidden) is still an expression of this love for others as well as of my love for God. And my sinful act (though secret) is an offense against this twofold love of God and neighbor — which in a sense is really one.

It has been said that unity is the eternal dream of God. Unity — oneness in the Spirit — is Christ's gift to his Church. By grievous ("mortal") sin I cut myself off from this union in the Spirit and offend against the community of the faithful. Reparation, therefore, is due to the Church as well as to Christ. This twofold reparation may find expression in and outside the sacrament of Christ's forgiveness. The situation outside the sacrament is perhaps fairly well understood: if I steal, I give back; if I hurt a reputation, I try to restore the good name I have damaged; if I give bad example, I try to repair the hurt done to another. Perhaps the situation of the sacrament is not so well understood, but for enriched Christian thinking it should be well understood indeed.

"Whose sins you shall forgive, they are forgiven," Christ tells his priests. So Christ has appointed

these priests to receive in his name
and in behalf of his Church our acts
of confessional humility — and, after
receiving these expressions, to ex-
tend his forgiveness to us and there-
by to restore us to the body of the
faithful which we have outraged by
our sin. If we offend someone,
we admit our fault: we apologize and
so endeavor, as far as we may, to
make things right. That is the necessary human way of things. In any
sin, we offend our neighbor as
well as God. And Christ, in institut-
ing the sacrament, has accepted
our human way and established that
we should acknowledge our faults
to a representative member of the
Church. So we are required to
confess our sins to a priest — a
fellow human being like ourselves —

as well as to Christ, when we acknowledge our guilt. Only in such a structure may we completely find the means of restoration suited to our hearts, to our whole person, in our quest for peace.

Awareness of the human factor in the priest, the representative of Christ and of his Church, will tend to urge itself upon us emphatically enough from the mere fact that the priest is there as we seek reconciliation. Perhaps what most of us need — and some of us need very greatly — is an awareness of Christ as present when we make our acts of humility and sorrow.

It is first and foremost Christ whom I have offended. It is he whom I have betrayed. It is he who has power in his own right to do away with sin, and it is because of this power that I may come at all to get forgiveness now in the sacrament.

Possibly it may be of help if I recall the incident of the woman who was "a sinner," who entered the house of Simon the Pharisee where Jesus was dining and cast herself in tears at his feet. She braved the public awareness of others who witnessed her act of sorrow and love at the feet of Christ. But the focus of her attention was on Christ, and she seemed in her sorrow and love rather oblivious of those around her. We know that she was then consoled with one of the most beautiful recorded manifestations of Christ's redeeming love: "Many sins are forgiven her because she has loved much. ... Your sins are forgiven you. ... Go in peace." If I can learn something of the humble love of the sinful woman and can, like her, keep the thought of Christ's love and mercy as an active awareness in my sorrow, it may help me greatly.

It is very good indeed if we can have a deep Christ-consciousness in relation to this sacrament and if we can put Christ actively and lovingly in the center of the picture when we receive it. (How would I proclaim my failures and express my sorrow if I were alone in the visual presence of the human Christ, whose love I have betrayed?)

Perhaps we may experience a meaningful and refreshing discovery in our lives if, through faith, we can let the image of the person of the priest who administers the sacrament diminish in our consciousness by relating ourselves humbly and lovingly to Christ in our avowals of guilt. It may help us greatly if our contrite acknowledgements of failure are made with the awareness that we are making them more than anything to the heart of Christ who will forgive us in and through his ministering priest.

If we can relate ourselves thus to Christ when we receive the sacrament, we may grow more and more to see how our preparations for receiving it may be meaningfully concerned with loving *contrition* for our offenses rather than a badgering of our wounded self ... and how our confession must be followed quite naturally with a loving gratitude to the forgiving Christ, who loves us very much in spite of our waywardness.

Our heartfelt contrition and humble gratitude, surely, should occupy a much greater place in our thinking about this sacrament than the mere avowal of guilt or the numbering of our lapses. We need, above all, to learn with contrition and gratitude to open our souls and receive the love and peace of Christ.

Ideally this sacrament should become for us from beginning to end a sacrament of peaceful joy. If it is not this way for us, we should strive to make it so.

And there is a much greater chance that we may make it so if we learn to overcome our fear and reluctance by approaching the sacrament in the true spirit — and if we learn to approach it more frequently rather than less frequently. Even weekly reception may be praiseworthy so long as it helps us — and there are many who may be helped greatly by weekly confession.

Though perhaps most people may not need it, some may find a rather complete catalog of possible failings to be of help. This aid is available; it is commonly issued under the title of "Examination of Conscience." Such a listing of faults has seemed a bit out of place in this little manual. But in the section which follows are given some thoughts which you may find helpful for reflection. It is hoped that you may find it meaningful to ponder them quietly as you think prayerfully at times of your responsibilities and ask yourself before God for a deeper insight into the trust he has given you as a wife and as a mother.

Thoughts for Prayerful Deliberation

(which should be read frequently and meditated deeply)

Parents should know and realize well that the Fourth Commandment applies extensively to them. The commandment, "Honor your father and your mother," imposes upon parents the grave obligation of deserving this "honor" in their manner of conducting themselves as parents.

.

I shall give an account to God for the souls of my children. This is no trifling matter.

.

Merely pointing out faults of my children is not enough.Well-directed parental correction that develops interior obedience is necessary.

·

I should know and understand well that without proper example on my part my words will be of little worth.

·

The task of a mother toward her children is not merely to correct faults but also to keep track of her children and give directives. The whereabouts of my child?... Companions? ... Activities? ... Where am I when my children return from school? — at home waiting for them? — and interested?

·

Children and school work: Here is an excellent area in which to build up character. Children are admonished by the Fourth Commandment to fulfill their school duties as directed; parents should take proper means to see that they do. ... The importance of a work schedule for a child — established and adhered to ...

·

My personal interest in the work and wholesome interests and activities of my children ... Assistance? ... Encouragement? ... Praise? ...

·

The religious education of my children — even from their earliest years ... The obligation is not a trifling one; I shall give an account to almighty God.

·

My children and Mass attendance ... My responsibility to see that they do attend — and my duty to give an example by reverent participation ...

·

Parental supervision of my children regarding their activities ... recreations ... choice of companions, etc. ... The home should be a place where my children feel invited to bring their companions; and it should be an attractive, wholesome place for them to enjoy recreation — properly regulated and supervised.

·

When my children come to me with questions and problems ... It is important that they should feel welcomed and encouraged. Patience and love can matter greatly here.

·

Cheerfulness and self-control on my part ... These may mean much to the emotional well-being and proper development of my child.

·

My duty of instructing children in proper manners — toward older people ... also, toward each other.

·

A mother's duty of nursing her child unless there is a justifying reason not to — and my regard for it ... A mother's duty to see that her children are baptized without unreasonable delay ...

·

My children and their vocation in life ... This is a matter primarily between God and my child: it is important that I be helpful in any way that a mother may — especially by my example and prayer — but also that I never interfere with God's way or endeavor to force my will toward the choice of a particular state — religious, married, single.

·

The duty of seeing that my child is prepared at the proper age for confession and Communion ...

·

My child's faith and the company that I permit or encourage ... There is a very real and delicate responsibility here.

·

My home ... It is highly important that I endeavor to make it an attractive, cheerful place for my husband and my children.

·

It should not be forgotten that the attitude I manifest toward my husband may greatly influence authority in the home. The children may learn much from my manifest attitude. It is important that what they learn should be good.

.

Above all, children should not be witness to angry words between parents. Sometimes the great virtue asked of me may be silence — a patient and cheerful (not angry) silence.

.

My husband's job of providing and managing family affairs may be vexing and worrisome. The home as an attractive place when he returns from work ... My readiness to share his concerns... Words of encouragement — and of praise at times ... The tenderness of understanding

201

and wifely affection when he is worried or discouraged ...

·

Nagging can never do anything but effect destruction and promote discord. The need of cheerful silence, at times — and of patience ...

·

"Two in one flesh" is God's plan for man and wife. When my husband looks to me for affection — even though I may be tired or distressed — I must know that in a true sense I am a part of him, as he of me. Real selflessness and generosity at times is called for. My response? ... My gentleness and tenderness? ...

·

The attractiveness of my person — even inside the home ... In the morning—before my husband leaves for work ... a nourishing breakfast according to his preferences? My appearance in serving it ... attractive? — and cheerful? When my husband returns from work, an attractive, pleasant appearance on my part can mean much.

.

The barrier of sulkiness — and above all of an angry and antagonized silence — if I have been crossed, or if there have been differences between my husband and me ... This tends to be highly destructive of marriage. "Two in one flesh" ... Differences must be mended, not aggravated. "Halfway" is not enough. I must learn to yield sweetly at times. Gentleness, affection, and patience, joined to humble prayer, may sometimes teach me much that is needed here.

Holy Mass: the Mystery of the Eucharist

The Eucharistic Celebration is a joyful event — a celebration of Christ's triumph ... and of our triumph in Christ. It is truly a banquet of love and joy, an intimate communion between Christ and the worshiping community. But it is more. It celebrates Christ's triumph over sin — my sin. And his triumph meant his passion and death for me. So the Eucharist makes a bid for joy, not hilarity. And my joy in the celebration will be definitely proportioned to my humble love and gratitude for the suffering love of Christ for me, which is commemorated in the memorial we celebrate.

The *Constitution on the Liturgy* says of the Mass:

"At the Last Supper, on the night on which he was betrayed, our Savior instituted the Eucharistic Sacrifice of his body and blood. This he did in order to perpetuate the Sacrifice of the Cross until he should come and that he might thus bestow upon his beloved spouse the Church a memorial of his death and resurrection: a sacrament of love, a sign of unity, a bond of charity—a paschal banquet in which Christ becomes our nourishment, the mind is filled with grace, and a pledge of future glory is given us."

At Mass, the followers of the Lord meet in a fellowship of worshipful love to celebrate in union with him the death and resurrection which is our forgiveness and our life.

On Calvary, Christ, the God-man, offered the sacrifice of his suffering self to the Father as a victim for our sin—to render an adequate reparation for the indignities of our sinful rebellion against our Maker.

At the supper on the night before he died, Christ looked forward to his sufferings of Calvary and to his glorious resurrection and, in anticipation, offered himself suffering and triumphant ("This is my body, which will be given up for you." "This is the cup of my blood ... It will be shed for you"). Then he gave himself — body, blood, soul, and divinity—to his disciples in the Eucharist, through which they were brought into an intimate communion with him, their redeeming Lord, in this celebration of the first Mass. In this Mass Christ was both priest (offerer) and victim (offered).

He has told us, the community of the faithful, to do what he then did. At the supper, he looked to the day ahead and offered the paschal mystery about to be enacted. We are told to make this same act of offering to the Father in union with him now glorious and triumphant. We are thus allowed to make Christ's offering our offering. When we do this, we celebrate the Mass: we proclaim again the death of the risen Christ.

Christ was priest and victim (because offerer and offered) at the Last Supper and at Calvary. He is, for the same reason, priest and glorified victim in our Mass. But we, too, are priests (we are baptized to this); and we exercise our priesthood when we, together with Christ, offer him, the conquering victim for us, in the celebration of the Mass.

Since the Mass is truly "a sign of unity, a bond of charity," it is quite fitting that after the Entrance Song and the Greeting we should make a Penitential Act together with the priest, contritely acknowledging in the presence of one another our sinfulness, which is disruptive of unity and charity in Christ.

A striving for fellowship in the worshiping community especially marks the *Liturgy of the Word*. It is in this that we may realize ourselves as a family united in our belief and way in Christ: "One Lord, one faith, one baptism." We strive here to enter into the spirit of Christ's own Eucharistic prayer for unity in order that we may be truly one in him.

So it is through our words spoken in loving penitence, and through speech again in the proclamation of the Word, that we express our striving for a unity of love and fellowship as we initiate our worship in the Mass.

But, as we enter into the Liturgy of the Eucharist itself, we add to our words an *act* which will physically express for us a union with Christ and with one another. This act begins as a symbolic expression of oneness as a community and looks forward to the sacrificial offering of Christ — and of ourselves through and in Christ.

As we enter upon this phase of the Eucharistic Sacrifice, we present a gift — material and of small value. It represents self, of course. But it also represents our union of charity with one another in Christ. We offer it together.

In our gift, one bread is presented, composed of many grains of wheat; one wine, from many grapes. It is presented by us — many individuals, but united in a fellowship of life and love and worship. In this one offering we have a union of wills: togetherness is emphasized.

In our presenting of the gifts of bread and wine, there is contained — as in every gift — an element of *self*.

And, just as at the Consecration our poor gifts of bread and wine become the priceless offering of Christ-the-Gift to the Father, so, too, at the Consecration our ordinary personal acts, which we now relate to the sacrificial offering of the Mass, take on a special splendor and value in Christ, the triumphant victim: and they become an offering of worth, acceptable to God the Father.

So the *Constitution on the Church* reminds us regarding the faithful worshipfully united at the celebration of the Eucharist that "all their works, prayers, and apostolic endeavors; their married and family life, their daily toil, and their recreations — if these are carried out under the direction of the Spirit—and even the painful aspects of life if patiently borne, will become a spiritual sacrifice, pleasing to God through Christ Jesus. And in the celebration of the Eucharist these are devoutly offered to the Father together with the body of the Lord. And so the laity, doing all things in holy adoration, consecrate the very world to God."

It is good if we appreciate deeply, very deeply, what Christ offers — and what we are invited to offer to the Father with and in him as a gift of very high value.

What does Christ offer? He offers, first, his atoning death and all that it represented. As Christ looked ahead to the morrow on that last evening with his apostles and reflected upon his sufferings and death about to take place, he referred to this sacrifice of self as the act in which he was to be "glorified" by the Father from whose will he had received his redemptive mission. And we may well ask as we contemplate his suffering with something of an understandable horror why this shattering episode in his life could merit such an acclaim from Christ's lips— a "glorification." The reason is this: Christ's offering was not Calvary alone; it was the glory of Easter and his resurrection as well. It is this to which we join the offering of our works and of ourselves.

In connection with this it is helpful to recall all that was involved in Christ's offering on Calvary. It is true that it was the offering of his death in all its particulars as the Father had willed it. But it is good to

remember that, in our total surrender in that final moment which we
term "death," there is represented
the totality of the life of any indi-
vidual. Our life from its earliest
beginning to the very end may be
considered very properly either as
living or as dying, depending on
whether we consider it creatively
as representing life-filled activity or
consider it as a continuing approach
to our inevitable term of this activity
upon earth. But, however we consider it, the totality of worth in my
living is represented at one specific
moment — that supreme moment
which is my "death."

So Christ's whole life was represented — its weariness, its zeal, its love,
its sufferings — from beginning to
end in his final act of surrender in

obedience to the Father. And, as I join my offering to that of Christ in the Eucharistic Sacrifice, I may bring the greatest meaning there if I offer the totality of my life in loving union with that of Christ — including all the sufferings, joys, loves, and material frustrations that shall be mine. This I do well to offer in a full surrender of myself to the will of the Father.

And each time I offer this, I have that additional and perhaps greatest offering of all to make, if I will make it. It is a childlike acceptance of the death that shall be mine — wherever, whenever, however the Father shall desire it — in submissive love and humility before the divine will that has decreed it for me. This is my act of love. This is my loving union

with Christ in my participation in
the Eucharistic Sacrifice. It is good
indeed if I can make it with a full
heart.

Perhaps Saint Paul is more than
hinting at this final factor of my
offering when he speaks of the
Eucharist and reminds us, "As
often as you shall eat this bread
and drink this cup, you proclaim
the death of the Lord *until he
comes*."

The Lord with whom we offer this
sacrifice is a living Lord — risen and
glorified. He is the pledge of our
own resurrection. And our offering
is a union with him that reaches out
hopefully and with assurance to our
companionship with him who *shall
come* and has already prepared a
place for us. ... And with this

thought we approach the completion of the Eucharistic Sacrifice.

Christ's redemptive work — his acceptance of us, and the union granted us in him — renders us acceptable to the Father. The gift of our works and of ourselves is incorporated in Christ's self-giving and is offered as something of a "package" gift with his own, which, because Christ offers it with us and for us, the Father will not refuse. It is a gift of love; it is all we can give. We give Christ, and we have by incorporation become something of a part of this Christ-gift to the Father.

The Father responds, as love always seeks to respond, with a return gift. Our gift was in Christ the mediator;

the Father returns a gift in Christ the mediator. The return gift of the Father to us in Christ is expressed in the Eucharistic Banquet, or Communion. In this Communion we may know an intimate union with Christ. Through, with, and in this union with Christ we should find, too, a deep union with the most holy Trinity, and a union in charity and fellowship with one another. Such union should indeed speak convincingly to the discerning mind and heart that Christ is all in all.

This is the Mass, the mystery of the Eucharist, "a sacrament of love, a sign of unity, a bond of charity," which we are permitted to celebrate with Christ — and which invites us in each celebration to look forward confidently in love *"until he comes."*